HOW DOES A ROCKET WORK?

Y0-AAB-728

WHAT DOES IT MEAN TO FLY-BY-WIRE?

Why does a man in space weigh nothing?

IS IT HOT OR COLD IN SPACE?

What was the first satellite to orbit in space?

How will men get to the moon?

What does an astronaut eat in space?

AIRPLANE FLY IN SPACE?

WHO CAN BECOME AN ASTRONAUT?

EACH OTHER THROUGH RADIOS?

HOW WILL ASTRONAUTS EXIST ON THE MOON?

A BLUE SKY?

What was the first American space satellite?

THE QUESTION AND ANSWER

RANDOM HOUSE

★ BOOK OF SPACE ★

Is there anything alive out in space?

falling back to earth?

Why does an astronaut see more than one sunset and sunrise in one day?

THE QUESTION AND ANSWER BOOK OF
SPACE

By RUTH A. SONNEBORN
Illustrated by JOHN POLGREEN

RANDOM HOUSE

Random House · New York

For David
who has been waiting impatiently
for what he calls "my book."

This title was originally cataloged by the Library of Congress as follows:
Sonneborn, Ruth A.   The Question and answer book of space. Illus. by John Polgreen. Random House ©1965   69p col illus photos   Answers to questions about space, rockets and satellites, spaceships, astronauts, a trip to the moon and space stations. Includes quiz section of chronological "firsts" by space travelers.   1 Rockets (Aeronautics) 2 Space flight I. Title   629.4   ISBN 0-394-80779-0   0-394-90779-5 (lib. bdg.)

Revised Edition

Manufactured in the United States of America

Photograph credits: A.T.&T. Photo, 30; Lick Observatory, University of California, 48; Mount Wilson and Palomar Observatories, 51. All other photographs from National Aeronautics and Space Administration.

CONTENTS

About Space

WHAT IS SPACE?

Space is the vast and limitless expanse that is all around us. Our earth is traveling in space, and so are the sun, the moon, the planets and the stars. There are many millions of heavenly bodies in space. Some are little particles like specks of dust. Others are so big that, compared to them, the earth would seem very tiny.

It is easy to think of stars in space. But because you are on the earth, it may not be as easy to think of the earth in space.

If you were an astronaut and could travel far away from the earth, you would see that the earth, too, is most certainly in space.

WHERE DOES SPACE BEGIN?

Our earth is a whirling body in space. And because you live on the earth, you are living in space. But when we talk about going *out* to space we mean traveling far, far away from earth — into what is sometimes called outer space.

Scientists do not agree on how many miles away from earth outer space begins. Some say it begins fifty miles away. Some say eight hundred. But scientists agree that to reach outer space we must go beyond our atmosphere.

Since space is all around the earth, we must never say we are going *up* to space. We must say we are going *out* to space.

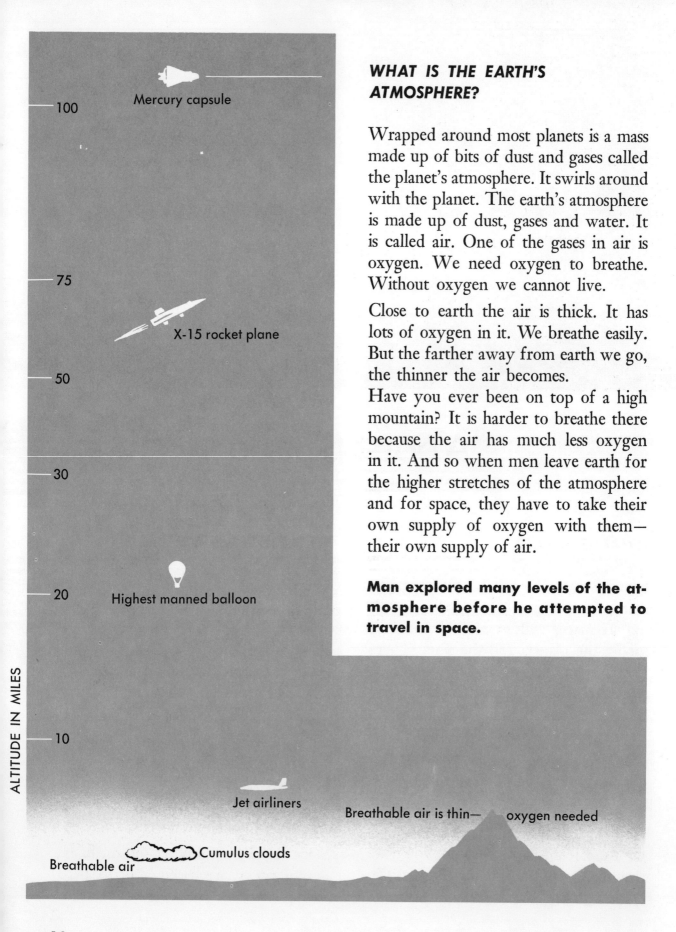

ALTITUDE IN MILES

100 — Mercury capsule

75 —

X-15 rocket plane

50 —

30 —

20 — Highest manned balloon

10 —

Jet airliners

Breathable air is thin—   oxygen needed

Cumulus clouds

Breathable air

WHAT IS THE EARTH'S ATMOSPHERE?

Wrapped around most planets is a mass made up of bits of dust and gases called the planet's atmosphere. It swirls around with the planet. The earth's atmosphere is made up of dust, gases and water. It is called air. One of the gases in air is oxygen. We need oxygen to breathe. Without oxygen we cannot live.

Close to earth the air is thick. It has lots of oxygen in it. We breathe easily. But the farther away from earth we go, the thinner the air becomes.

Have you ever been on top of a high mountain? It is harder to breathe there because the air has much less oxygen in it. And so when men leave earth for the higher stretches of the atmosphere and for space, they have to take their own supply of oxygen with them— their own supply of air.

Man explored many levels of the atmosphere before he attempted to travel in space.

CAN YOU SEE SPACE?

In the daytime, when you look away from earth, you see clouds, blue sky, bright sunlight. You do not see space. But you can see some objects in space such as the moon, on certain clear days. Between you and space there is a bright curtain of light that makes it hard for you to see beyond it.

The sun's rays stream through the atmosphere. They strike against particles and bits of dust. The rays light up these particles and the particles scatter the light all around the atmosphere. Some of it looks blue to us—the sky. Some of it looks yellow—the sunbeams. This scattered light keeps you from seeing faraway space.

But on a clear night when the sun has gone, you look up. You see stars, planets, perhaps the moon. You see blackness all around them. You see space.

WHERE DOES SPACE END?

Nobody knows.
We know that the earth, the sun, the moon, the planets—the whirling bodies we call our solar system—take up only a very small part of space. Through our most powerful telescopes we can see stars that look tiny because they are billions and billions and billions of miles away from earth.

But what lies beyond? We cannot see. We do not know. Perhaps there is no end to space at all.

Part of the earth as it looks to an astronaut in space. Looking out of his spaceship, the astronaut may see white clouds over a blue ocean and on the horizon. The

DOES AN ASTRONAUT SEE A BLUE SKY?

The astronaut out in space looks *away* from earth. He does not see sky. The sky is part of the earth's atmosphere and the astronaut is far, far beyond the atmosphere.

The sky looks blue to us on earth when the blue-green-violet colors of the sun-

light strike the tiny dust particles in the atmosphere. The other colors of sunlight stream through to earth, but the blue-green-violet rays are scattered about overhead. This makes our sky look blue. The astronaut looks out of his spaceship window *away* from earth and even in the daytime he sees blackness all around.

In the blackness he sees thousands of brilliant stars, the flashing sun, and sometimes the silvery moon. But when he looks toward the earth, he sees a blue band encircling it. He sees the sky.

WHY DOES SPACE LOOK BLACK TO AN ASTRONAUT?

The sun's rays create light that we can see only when they strike an object and are reflected from it. We call this visible light.

Sunlight streams to us on earth through the thick dust-filled atmosphere. The

Scott Carpenter took this dramatic photograph of the blue band around the earth as the sun was setting.

atmosphere that surrounds the earth appears as a hazy blue band. Beyond—looking away from earth—he sees the star-filled blackness of space.

light strikes every tiny bit of dust. It is reflected from each of them, and is scattered around everywhere.

But sunlight streams swiftly through space without scattering light. It lights up the moon, the planets, the stars, all objects in space. Surrounding them there is no visible light. And so space looks black to the astronaut, when he looks out of his spaceship window away from the earth.

IS IT HOT OR COLD IN SPACE?

Everything whirling in space is hot or cold or in between. Stars are huge furnaces. When rays stream out from them and reach any object in space, they heat it.

The sun is the star that warms our earth and the other planets. These heavenly bodies reflect heat just as they reflect light. Near a star or a hot planet, space is

hot. The farther one gets from them, the colder it is. Most of space is very cold.

IS THERE NOISE IN SPACE?

There is no noise that human beings can hear. Sounds on earth make waves in the air and these waves carry the sounds to our ears. But there is no air in space. And so, to the human ear, space is absolutely quiet.

ARE THERE CLOUDS IN SPACE?

There are no clouds in space. There is no water. Clouds are made up of water and bits of dust. Without water clouds cannot form.

The photographs of clouds that satellites take out in space are part of the earth's atmosphere and have been taken many, many miles beyond those clouds.

ARE THERE DANGEROUS RAYS IN SPACE?

Space is full of dangerous rays. Most of them are cosmic rays. They are streams of electrical particles, so small you cannot see them. They radiate or shoot out from the sun and the stars, and travel in all directions as fast as light travels.

Only a small number of cosmic rays pierce the solid walls of a spaceship, and they arrive inside so weakened that they are generally harmless.

DO RAYS FROM SPACE REACH THE EARTH?

Some rays do reach the earth but luckily for us these rays are no longer dangerous by the time they arrive.

Magnetism pulls the rays toward the earth. But most of them are trapped in a giant electrical zone that encircles the earth. This is the Van Allen Radiation Belt, named after the man who discovered it.

The few rays that escape the trap to straggle through to earth are so weak when they reach earth, that they are no longer harmful.

WHAT DOES A GEIGER COUNTER COUNT IN SPACE?

The Geiger counter is a detective in space just as it is on earth. In space it detects the presence of cosmic rays by discovering the ions, the tiny electrical particles that make up these rays.

The Geiger counter clicks when ions are near. It measures them. A loud, fast click means a strong ion. A low, slow click means a weak ion. It counts the ions. The needle on the dial swings around and points to the number of ions it has counted. And the Geiger counter also discovers and reports the direction in which the cosmic ray is traveling.

Cutaway diagram of the Van Allen Radiation Belt which encircles the earth. To avoid passing through this belt, manned spacecraft can be launched through escape zones.

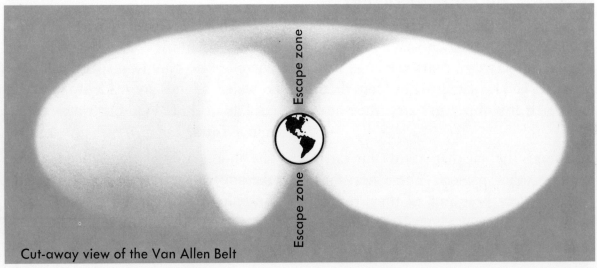

Escape zone

Escape zone

Cut-away view of the Van Allen Belt

WHY DOES MAN WANT TO EXPLORE SPACE?

Man has always been an explorer. From the beginning of time he has searched to learn more about what lies close to him and what lies far away from him. Man has explored space for only a very few years, but already we have gathered a great amount of information from satellites and manned spaceships. Inside these ships cameras and instruments record, measure and report their findings in space. And astronauts describe sights never before seen. We are learning new facts about the stars, the planets, the sun, the moon, our own earth.

Scientists hope that man's successful landings on the moon will lead to a breakthrough. They believe that from the moon they may find answers to such questions as: How did the earth come into being? Was the moon ever a part of our earth? Or was it a former planet that wandered too close to the earth billions of years ago and got caught in the earth's gravitational field? Or was the moon created at the same time as the earth?

How were the planets, the stars, the sun born? How did life on earth start? Are there other worlds like ours out in space?

In their search for answers scientists are busily studying the first samples of rocks and soil brought back from the moon. They hope to find out if the moon is a cold, dead mass or if it has a molten interior that produces volcanic activity similar to that on earth.

A Mariner approaches Mars, equipped to send close-up pictures back to earth.

IS THERE ANYTHING ALIVE OUT IN SPACE?

Are there living plants, animals, human beings? Does anything or anybody live on a planet out in space?

These are exciting questions that man has been puzzling over for years. Now that we know how to reach space, will we soon find the answers?

Many scientists think there may be some form of life on the planet Mars, although the atmosphere around it is not like the earth's. After the moon, Mars may be the first planet to be visited by man in our space program.

A series of satellites, the Mariners, are being sent out toward Mars to take clear close-up pictures and record important measurements. Mariner 4, after traveling from earth for seven and a half months, sent back the first pictures of Mars.

In another program scientists have tried to discover if there is intelligent life in space by sending messages out to space and listening for messages from space. They use powerful radios and huge devices, called antenna dishes, to catch incoming sounds.

The fascinating search goes on. Perhaps by the time you grow up we will know whether there is anything or anybody living on other planets in space.

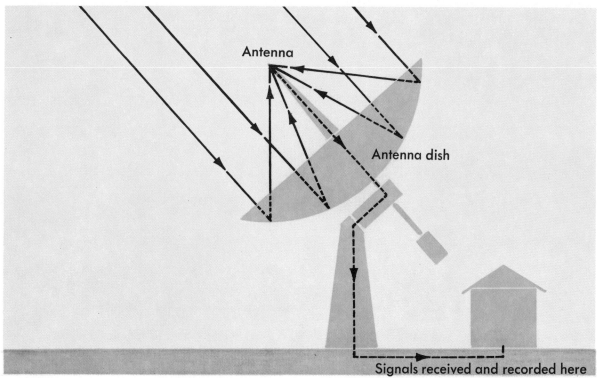

Antenna

Antenna dish

Signals received and recorded here

Antenna dish of a radio telescope picks up radio signals from outer space and focuses them on the antenna. The signals are amplified and sent to a recorder where their strength is traced on a moving strip of paper and can be studied. (See photograph on p. 19.)

WHY CAN'T AN AIRPLANE FLY IN SPACE?

Some airplanes have propeller engines and some have jet engines. Both suck in air and burn it with gasoline for power.

Space is the region beyond earth without air. Therefore, an *air*plane cannot fly in space; its engines cannot work there. And, of course, without air the plane's wings could not give lift. Lift is a rising force caused by air flowing over the wings.

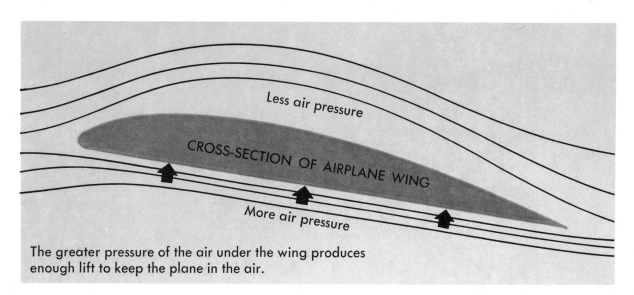

Less air pressure

CROSS-SECTION OF AIRPLANE WING

More air pressure

The greater pressure of the air under the wing produces enough lift to keep the plane in the air.

About Rockets, Satellites and Spaceships

WHAT IS A SPACEPORT?

A spaceport is a special kind of city where every building is used to plan and carry out the exploring of space. In the huge buildings spaceships are assembled. There are machine shops for making repairs. There are big storage tanks filled with fuel for rockets. There are huge tractors, trains, and barges to move the giant ships and rockets around, and special buildings to house them and protect them from weather.

There is the blockhouse for the men who control the timing of a launching. There is a weather station to check minute-by-minute weather conditions before a launching. And, of course, there are the huge launching pads from which satellites and spaceships are sent off to space.

There are radio and radar stations, computer centers where problems can be solved quickly, an observatory where engineers can watch a launching with safety.

A spaceport is truly a new kind of city, a place on earth where space journeys begin.

Atlas rocket launch at Cape Kennedy. Launching pads, spread over a distance of many miles, are ready and waiting for future blast-offs.

A blockhouse at Cape Kennedy—the control center for the launching of a rocket.

A radio telescope in the spaceport. This tracks the path of a satellite.

The first stage of a Saturn rocket being lifted to the launching pad by a powerful hoist.

WHAT IS A GANTRY?

A gantry is a rolling service station for rockets and spaceships in a spaceport. Before blast-off it is moved out to the launching pad on tracks. Its powerful hoist lifts rockets, satellites and spaceships up on the high pad. Within its bright red and white steel frame there are elevators to carry the men who will check the machines during the countdown. On manned flights, the astronaut is carried up to the spacecraft in one of these elevators.

The gantry is a busy, crowded place until just a few minutes before blast-off. Then the service men run off the field and the gantry is rolled quickly away to the farthest end of the track.

WHAT IS A PAYLOAD?

A payload may be a satellite. It may be a spaceship. It may be a missile. It may even be fireworks, a shower of green, red, blue, golden stars in the sky on a holiday like the 4th of July. A payload is whatever a rocket carries away from earth.

Rocket in place on launching pad is being checked by men in the gantry. The countdown has begun.

All lights flash green as firing time approaches. These are tense moments inside the blockhouse.

WHAT HAPPENS DURING A COUNTDOWN?

A countdown is a check-up time before a launching. Before a launching from earth, a loudspeaker booms out the time from the blockhouse. The countdown begins in minutes and ends in seconds. "T (Time) minus 480"—this means 480 minutes or 8 hours of countdown.

A crew high up in the gantry carries out a very careful check of every inch and part of the rocket and spaceship perched on the launching pad. Inside the blockhouse the test conductor calls out orders to the crew. He names each part to be checked. Alongside of him sit engineer-monitors in front of rows of dials. If the result is satisfactory the monitor pushes a button which turns on a green light. If the result is not satisfactory the countdown is halted. The loudspeaker stops booming. It starts counting again when a green light shows that the correction has been made.

A countdown may take hours or even days. It will continue until all dials flash green. The last minute sounds out in seconds, "T minus 60, T minus 59, T minus 58" until finally the loudspeaker booms, "10—9—8—7—6—5—4—3—2—1—ZERO!" The test conductor pushes the firing button, and with a loud roar the rocket blasts off.

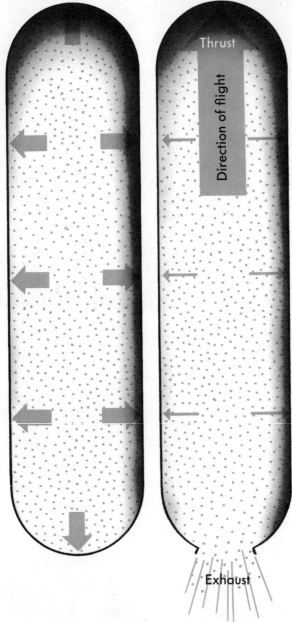

In a closed container (left), molecules of air push against all sides with equal pressure. In a rocket (right), molecules of air escape through the tail. Pressure at the nose is greater.

HOW DOES A ROCKET WORK?

A rocket is a powerful engine that carries a satellite or a spaceship off the earth out to space. It is built with a narrow opening at the tail. A special kind of fuel is placed inside the rocket. This fuel is set on fire. It burns rapidly and expands into very hot gases. The hot gases rush around inside the rocket and press hard against the solid walls. But at the tail they have no wall to push against. They escape through the opening. There is no force or pressure at the tail to balance the push of the gases pressing against the nose of the rocket. The force of the gases pushing against the nose is greater than that of the gases escaping at the tail. It is this push—called thrust—that causes the rocket to move *opposite* to the direction of the escaping gases. Thrust starts a rocket on its journey into space.

You can see how a rocket works by trying this experiment with an ordinary balloon. Blow it up full of air. Then let it go quickly. It will fly out of your hand. The air rushing out of the balloon gives the air inside a chance to push harder. And away the balloon zips.

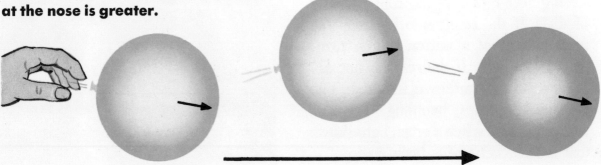

HOW LONG DOES IT TAKE A ROCKET TO REACH SPACE?

It may take only five minutes for a rocket to reach space. It starts off from earth moving slowly. As it rises it travels faster and faster. Usually it will reach a speed of about 18,000 miles per hour going into orbit around the earth. This speed is about 300 times as fast as a car is allowed to go on a high-speed highway.

WHAT IS A SATELLITE?

Astronomers call our moon a satellite of the earth. They call it a satellite because the word means a follower, an attendant. The moon travels in orbit around the earth. It is our follower. The earth, too, is a satellite—a satellite of the sun. It moves in orbit around the sun.

The machines we send out into orbit around us in space are also called satellites. They are true satellites of the earth because, like the moon, they travel in a path around it.

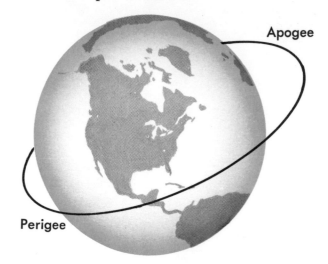

Orbit of an artificial earth satellite. The point in the orbit that is nearest the earth is called the perigee. The point farthest from earth is the apogee.

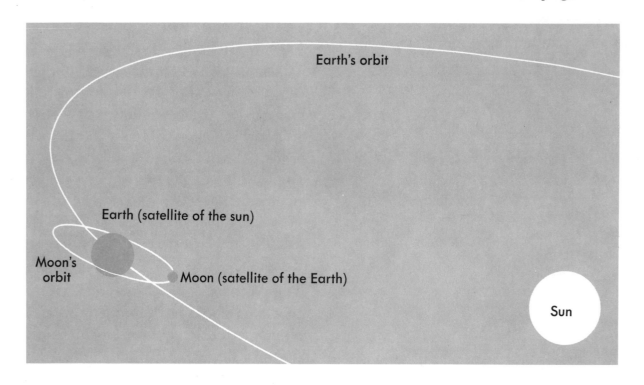

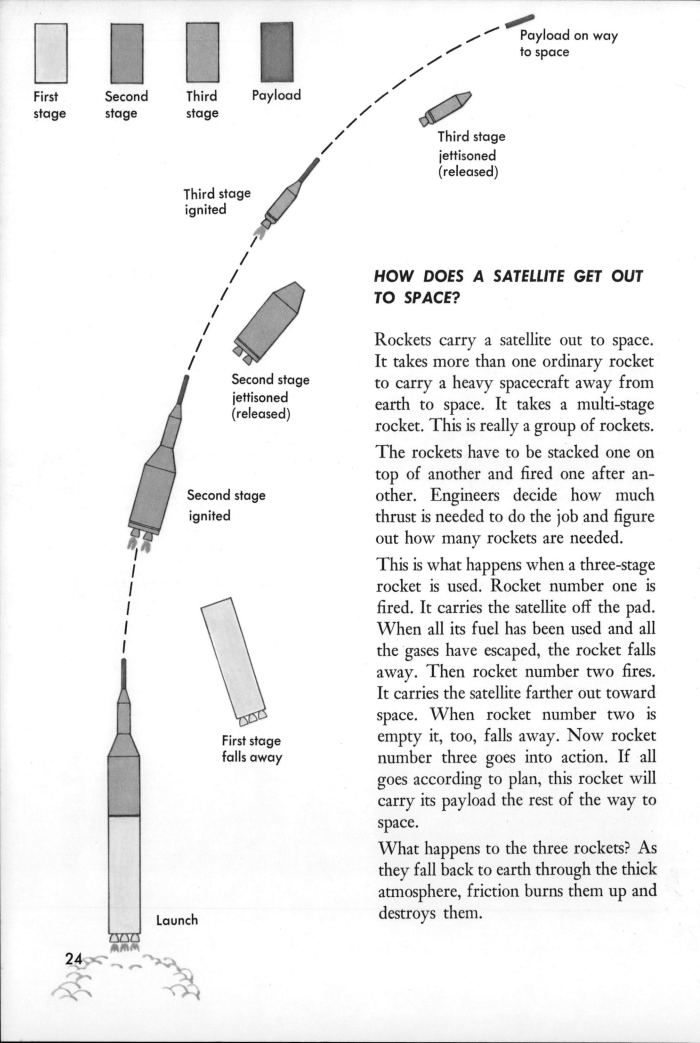

First
stage

Second
stage

Third
stage

Payload

Payload on way
to space

Third stage
jettisoned
(released)

Third stage
ignited

Second stage
jettisoned
(released)

Second stage
ignited

First stage
falls away

Launch

24

HOW DOES A SATELLITE GET OUT TO SPACE?

Rockets carry a satellite out to space. It takes more than one ordinary rocket to carry a heavy spacecraft away from earth to space. It takes a multi-stage rocket. This is really a group of rockets.

The rockets have to be stacked one on top of another and fired one after another. Engineers decide how much thrust is needed to do the job and figure out how many rockets are needed.

This is what happens when a three-stage rocket is used. Rocket number one is fired. It carries the satellite off the pad. When all its fuel has been used and all the gases have escaped, the rocket falls away. Then rocket number two fires. It carries the satellite farther out toward space. When rocket number two is empty it, too, falls away. Now rocket number three goes into action. If all goes according to plan, this rocket will carry its payload the rest of the way to space.

What happens to the three rockets? As they fall back to earth through the thick atmosphere, friction burns them up and destroys them.

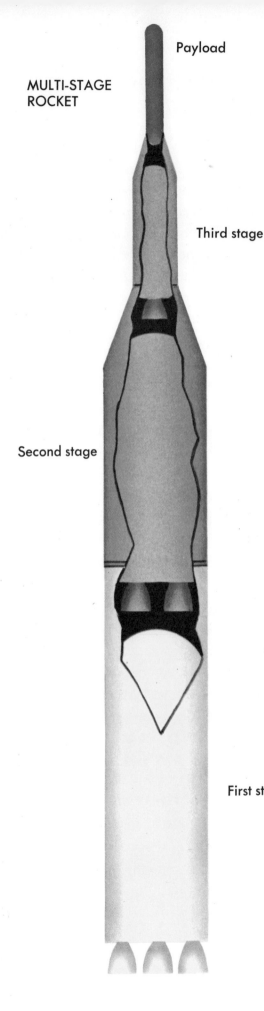

Payload

MULTI-STAGE
ROCKET

Third stage

Second stage

First stage

A tracking station picks up signals from an orbiting satellite.

HOW DO WE KNOW WHERE A SATELLITE IS IN SPACE?

A network of tracking stations is set up in carefully chosen spots around the world to keep track of man-made satellites. As a satellite orbits, it sends out continuous *beep, beep, beeps*. Engineers at the tracking stations listen for these sounds on receiving sets. They can tell when a satellite is approaching, when it is directly overhead, and when it is leaving their part of the world. This information is reported to a tracking headquarters, where computers chart the satellite's path.

If the satellite is a manned spaceship, men in the tracking stations can carry on conversations with the astronaut. They can learn what he sees in space, how his ship is performing, and how his body is reacting to the special conditions of space travel.

WHAT KEEPS A SATELLITE FROM FALLING BACK TO EARTH?

Did you ever whirl a skipping rope around and around over your head? The rope stretches out straight and smooth. The wooden handle moves in an even path overhead. It moves in an orbit. You can feel the force of the speeding handle as it pulls to escape from you. But you and the rope pull the handle just hard enough to keep it in orbit.

Very much the same thing happens with a satellite. If nothing held it back, it would escape from the earth orbit. But gravity constantly pulls on the satellite. The balance of the gravity force and the force pushing the satellite toward escape keeps it in orbit. Engineers figure out how fast to make the satellite whirl around the earth. The satellite must travel at the right speed to prevent gravity from pulling it back to earth and at the right speed to keep it from flying out of the earth orbit.

CAN A SATELLITE ORBIT IN A PERFECT CIRCLE?

If the earth were perfectly round and uniform, gravity would pull with even strength on a satellite in orbit. The satellite would travel in a perfect circle. But the earth is not perfectly round and uniform. As the satellite travels around the earth, gravity pulls it with varying force. This force makes a satellite travel in an egg-shaped path, called an ellipse.

Engineers, however, can control the shape of the orbit before a satellite is launched. And man has learned how to change the shape and position of the orbit of a spacecraft while in flight.

HOW LONG WILL A SATELLITE ORBIT IN SPACE?

A satellite will keep on orbiting in space until something slows it up. If this happens gravity will pull the satellite out of orbit back to earth.

But what is there in space to slow up a satellite? There is no air to create friction, nothing to act like a brake. However, if a satellite is in an orbit that swings close enough to earth to dip into the atmosphere, it will slow down a little bit each time it goes into the thin air. Eventually, it will be slowed up enough to be pulled out of orbit by gravity.

There are other moving bodies out in space. There is the very slight chance that one might collide with a satellite and cut down its speed. But space is so big that this is not likely to happen. Scientists predict that satellites now traveling in a path high enough to escape the atmosphere completely will continue in orbit forever.

Dipping into the earth's atmosphere makes the satellite travel more slowly. Gradually it will be pulled back to earth by gravity.

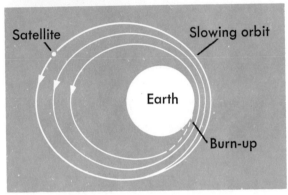

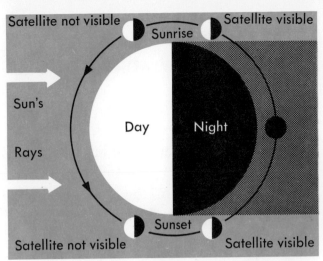

A satellite is visible when the side lighted by the sun's rays is viewed against a dark sky.

CAN YOU SEE A MAN-MADE SATELLITE IN SPACE WITHOUT A TELESCOPE?

There are some man-made satellites you can see without a telescope. You may see the Echo satellites, huge silvery balloons, made of plastic with a coating of shining aluminum. You may also see Pegasus without a telescope. When these satellites are at certain points of orbit in space, the sun's rays fall directly on them and light them up.

Some newspapers carry an item on the weather page headed VISIBLE SATELLITES. This tells you when you can see them. You will have to wait until after sundown or get up out of bed before

sunrise for the best view of them. It is then that they glow brightest, and it is then that you can watch them as they move more swiftly than the stars across the dark sky.

WHAT JOBS DO SATELLITES DO?

Satellites are space explorers and space researchers. They are our eyes and ears in space. They measure. They take pictures. They report back to earth what lies beyond the atmosphere. From them we learn about cosmic rays, the magnetic belt circling our earth, and streams of meteoroids. They give us close-up pictures of the planets and the sun, and even show the side of the moon we never see from earth.

Special satellites do special jobs. Communication satellites relay telephone and telegraph messages and TV programs. Navigation satellites send out information for air and sea travelers. Weather satellites take pictures of clouds for weather stations on earth.

WHAT DOES A WEATHER SATELLITE DO?

A weather satellite is often called a "weather eye" because as it orbits it sees the weather all the way around the earth. Tiros I was one of the first weather satellites. In 1960, during its first six months, it took some 22,000 television pictures and sent them back to earth.

Other Tiros satellites are now gathering information as they orbit in space. Tiros III, for example, photographed a hurricane. These pictures helped weather stations chart the path of the giant storm more accurately.

There is a constant flow of pictures and reports coming from our "weather

The spiral form of hurricane Hilda, photographed by a Tiros weather satellite.

eyes." Perhaps one day we will learn enough so that we can control the weather.

A Tiros weather satellite

HOW DOES A NAVIGATION SATELLITE HELP TRAVELERS?

Once the orbit of a navigation satellite has been established, the captain of a ship or the pilot of a plane can fix the exact position of his ship or plane by the radio signals he receives from the satellite.

When fog covers land and sea, and storms break contact with earth stations, captains and pilots depend on signals from these satellites to guide them safely home.

Transit IB is a navigation satellite. It has been in orbit since 1960.

A Telstar communication satellite

HOW DO COMMUNICATION SATELLITES WORK?

They can work in several ways:
1. Radio waves from one earth station can be *bounced* off a large satellite, such as an Echo sphere, to another earth station with a good receiver. In space, radio waves travel in a straight line, so the earth station and the satellite must be in a straight line to make the bounce work.

2. A satellite can carry a receiver and transmitter, catch the radio waves and strengthen them before it *relays* them to another earth station. This satellite must carry a lot of electronic equipment and a power system to relay radio waves. The Early Bird, Syncoms and Telstars work this way.

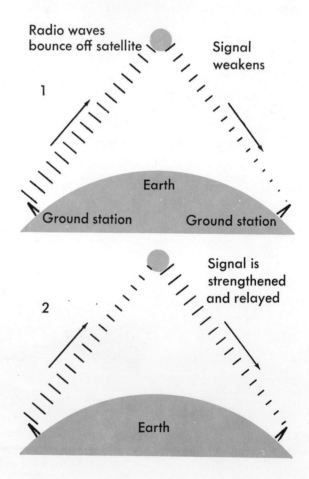

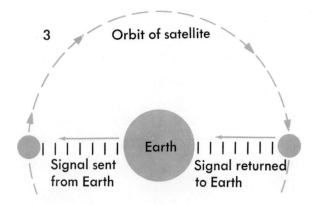

3. A satellite might also carry recording equipment to *store* information sent to it on one side of the earth. It will then transmit it to the other side of the earth in response to a signal sent from the ground or even from men in a space ship.

4. Three satellites placed high enough make it possible to transmit radio waves all around the world at once. Radio waves from the earth travel up to one satellite. That satellite relays them to the second, which in turn relays them to the third. The waves can be transmitted from each satellite to the earth beneath.

Radio waves can carry voice messages (telephone), television signals, or teletype information. With three high communication satellites, it will be possible to send television programs around the world. People everywhere will be able to see and hear the same program at the same time.

At 22,300 miles from earth, three communication satellites can send signals that will reach the whole world.

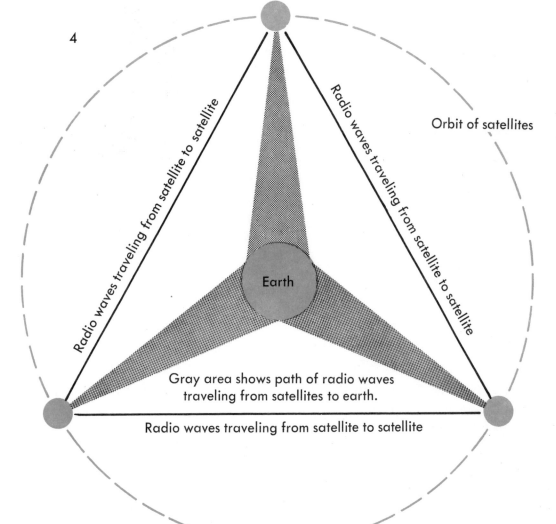

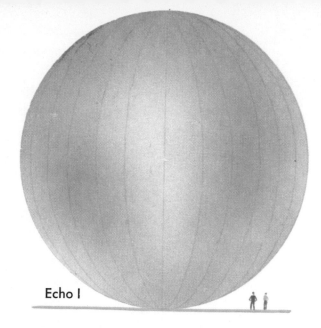

Echo I

Sputnik I orbited for four months. But because at one point of its orbit it dipped into the earth's atmosphere, it slowly lost speed. Then gravity pulled it toward the earth and the heat of friction destroyed it. But Sputnik I had proved to the world that man can reach into space.

Explorer I

HOW DOES A BALLOON SATELLITE GET OUT TO SPACE?

A balloon satellite, such as one of the Echoes, is sent out to space folded up in the nose of a rocket. Inside the folded balloon is a special kind of chemical. When the rocket reaches space, it hurls the balloon out of its nose into orbit around the earth. Soon the chemical becomes a gas. The gas swells. It inflates the balloon to its full size. Then the balloon behaves like any other satellite in space.

WHAT WAS THE FIRST SATELLITE TO ORBIT IN SPACE?

The world was thrilled when the Russians announced that Sputnik I was in orbit in space. This was on October 4th, 1957. The Russian word Sputnik means satellite or companion of the earth. Sputnik I carried scientific instruments to measure and report on temperature, air pressure, cosmic rays, and meteoroids. It was the first man-made satellite.

WHAT WAS THE FIRST AMERICAN SPACE SATELLITE?

Explorer I, launched from the coast of Florida on January 31st, 1958, was the first American space satellite. It reached space in seven minutes. Its Geiger counters detected a belt of radiation, called the Van Allen Belt, that surrounds the earth. Explorer I is still out in space orbiting around the earth.

Spacecraft

(Right) The capsule of the Gemini spacecraft provides cabin space for two men. When the flight is completed, the equipment section is left behind; only the capsule returns to earth.

(Left) The Gemini spacecraft in position atop a giant launch rocket.

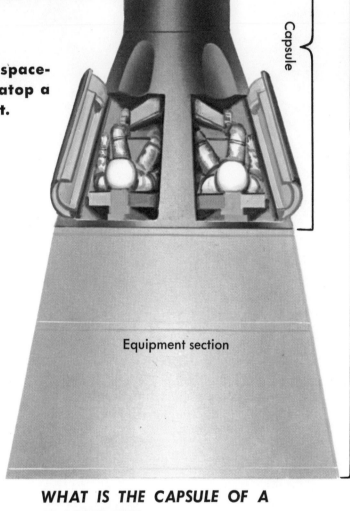

Capsule

Gemini spacecraft

Equipment section

TITAN II
ROCKET

WHAT IS THE CAPSULE OF A SPACECRAFT?

The capsule is the part of a spacecraft where the crew and instruments are carried. There the astronauts work, eat, sleep and live until they return from space to earth. If the capsule carries astronauts, it may be called the command module. Below the command module on some vehicles there is a service module to hold extra equipment such as fuel cells for electric power and tanks of oxygen for breathing.

33

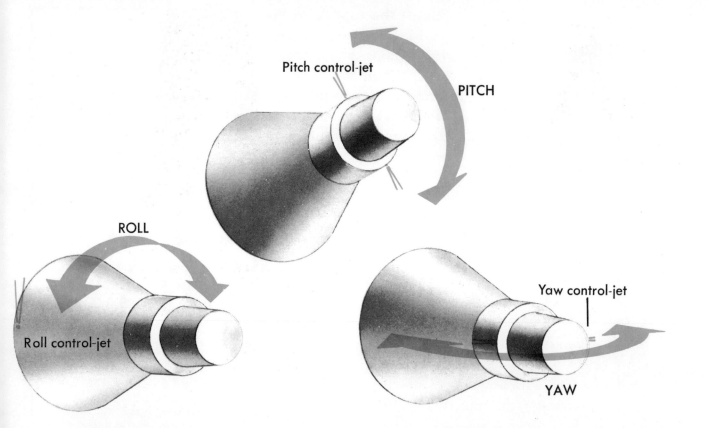

Pitch control-jet

PITCH

ROLL

Roll control-jet

Yaw control-jet

YAW

HOW DO ASTRONAUTS STEER A SPACESHIP?

Most of the time an astronaut does not need to steer his spaceship. Space is so big and there is so little traffic that he need not worry about collisions the way a motorist does. And his spaceship will keep in its orbit without his help. But when the time comes to rendezvous, dock, or land the ship, he must steer accurately.

Spaceships are equipped with devices called attitude control-jets. (These controls are set to work automatically but they can be operated by the astronaut.) They send out spurts of gas. As the gas spurts out it changes the direction of the ship. Some spurts make the ship yaw—turn to the left or to the right. Others pitch the nose of the ship either

up or down. Some make it roll from side to side. The ship can also be moved in any direction by thruster-rockets. Retro-rockets, too, help an astronaut steer by slowing up the ship. And so with attitude control-jets, retro-rockets, and thruster-rockets, astronauts will manage to do the exact steering needed for rendezvous, docking and returning to earth.

WHAT DOES IT MEAN TO FLY-BY-WIRE?

A spaceship has an automatic control system. An astronaut can lie on his space couch and be boosted to space and travel in space without lifting a finger. But if he wants or needs to take over control of the ship, he can fly-by-wire, which means he can use a control stick to send commands to the automatic system.

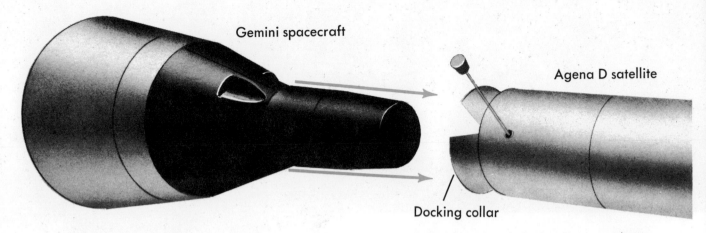

Gemini spacecraft

Agena D satellite

Docking collar

WHAT IS A RENDEZVOUS IN SPACE?

Rendezvous (pronounced **ron**-day-voo) is a French word. It means a meeting. So if you read about two ships holding a rendezvous in space, you know they are meeting. They meet and they dock. That means they join. A part of one ship slips into a special place in the other ship. They may, for instance, make a nose-to-nose docking.

One of the main purposes of Project Gemini was to learn to rendezvous and dock in space. Crews could then move from one craft to another. Rendezvousing and docking would be important operations in a successful moon expedition. Gemini 8 (March 16, 1966) performed the first docking with another vehicle in space.

To rendezvous and dock, the astronaut must be able to control the spaceship's attitude, speed, and orbit. Here, the nose of the Gemini is about to be slipped into the collar of an Agena satellite.

WHAT PULLS A SPACESHIP OUT OF ORBIT FOR A RETURN TO EARTH?

To stay in orbit a spaceship must travel at the right speed to balance the pull of gravity. To send the ship out of orbit for a return to earth, it is necessary to slow it down and destroy this balance.

A rocket, called a retro-rocket, is used to cut down the speed of the ship. This rocket, fired automatically or by the astronaut, acts like a brake. Immediately the ship loses speed, and gravity pulls it out of orbit, out of space, toward the earth.

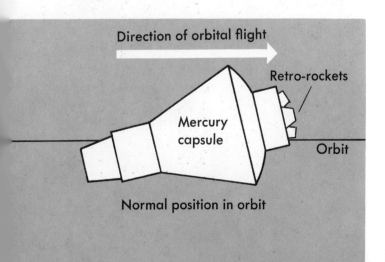

Direction of orbital flight

Retro-rockets

Mercury capsule

Orbit

Normal position in orbit

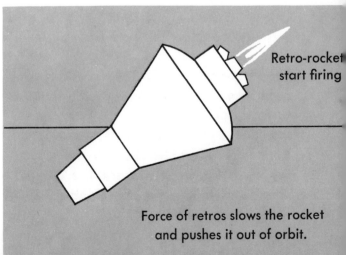

Retro-rocket start firing

Force of retros slows the rocket and pushes it out of orbit.

WHY IS THE TRIP BACK TO EARTH FIERY HOT?

The spaceship leaves space behind and plunges through the thick atmosphere toward the earth. The ship forces its way through air that becomes thicker and thicker as it nears the earth. The thick air rubs along the nose and sides of the ship. This creates friction, and friction creates heat. The ship grows hotter and hotter all the time. It glows with fiery heat. But inside, the astronaut is safe because the nose of the ship is covered with a special heat shield.

Friction also slows the ship down. Finally at just the right moment and just the right distance from earth a small parachute, called a drogue, opens out overhead. Soon a larger parachute opens out, too. The two parachutes drag on the ship, and it begins a gentle descent to a safe landing on the sea. Other devices are being tested for landing on the ground.

An astronaut safely rides a Mercury capsule as it streaks through the earth's atmosphere. The white-hot heat shield reaches a temperature of about 3000 degrees Fahrenheit. The astronaut, riding with his back toward the shield, sees an orange glow stretching out behind the capsule.

About Astronauts

WHO CAN BECOME AN ASTRONAUT?

Many men and women, too, in this country would like to become astronauts. But very few can pass the many difficult tests they must take in order to be chosen.

Today two kinds of astronauts are needed: pilot-astronauts to command the spaceships, and scientist-astronauts to carry on research during flight or on the moon or a planet.

An astronaut must be a United States citizen. To be a pilot, he must not be older than 35. A scientist-astronaut can be no older than 34. Men not more than six feet in height are preferred.

To be an astronaut, a man must have had a college education. Pilots must have studied engineering or some other science. Scientists must have studied engineering or medicine. They must have gone on to graduate school after college and proved themselves outstanding in their work. Of course, the pilot-astronaut must have had long experience as a flyer with at least 1000 hours of flying a jet airplane. All astronauts must be very healthy and intelligent. Above all, they must be the kind of people who live calmly and can solve problems in the face of danger.

HOW ARE ASTRONAUTS TESTED?

Men who wish to become astronauts get the kind of physical check-up the doctor gives you. And then they are given many other physical tests. New kinds of tests have been developed to try to discover how a man's body and a man's mind will behave in the new world of space.

Can he stand terrific heat? As a test, he spends two hours in a fiercely hot room. Can he take extreme cold? He must keep his feet in a bucket of ice water for seven minutes.

How do his lungs react to the kind of air he will breathe in the spaceship? To test this the astronaut spends hours in a special chamber.

What kind of man is he? Tense or relaxed? Calm or excitable? Able to be alone and think alone? And what are his reasons for wanting to become an astronaut?

It took many weeks of testing and studying the results of the tests, before the first seven American astronauts were selected.

WHY DO ASTRONAUTS GO TO SCHOOL?

They have been to college and some have been to military school. They have flown for many, many hours. Still they must go to school. They have a great deal to learn.

An astronaut must understand everything about the complicated workings of rockets and spaceships. He must know how to control and interpret the many research instruments the ship will carry. He must learn how to keep in touch with tracking stations around the world. And perhaps most important and most difficult of all, he must experience the unusual sensations he will feel while in flight. He must know how his body reacts to weightlessness and what it is like to feel very, very heavy.

If these feelings are not strange to him, they will not interfere with the many tasks he must carry out while he is in space. He needs new knowledge and he must acquire new skills to prepare him for the exciting adventure of traveling in space.

The first seven American astronauts. Front row, left to right: Walter M. Schirra, Jr., Donald K. Slayton, John H. Glenn, Jr. and M. Scott Carpenter. Back row, left to right: Alan B. Shepard, Jr., Virgil I. "Gus" Grissom and L. Gordon Cooper, Jr.

Everything inside a spaceship floats unless it is fastened down. This astronaut has a problem when he lets go of his camera.

DOES A MAN FEEL DIFFERENT IN SPACE THAN HE DOES ON EARTH?

He feels very different. On his space couch traveling with increasing speed away from earth, his body feels very, very heavy. He may feel as much as five times heavier than usual. Yet when his ship goes into orbit, his body feels light. He feels weightless. These are strange feelings for a human being. An astronaut must learn how to live with them.

WHY DOES A MAN IN SPACE WEIGH NOTHING?

To understand this you must understand why he has weight on earth. The earth pulls everything to it. It exerts a *gravity force*. We call the effect of this force on us or any object *weight*. To measure your weight in pounds you step on a scale. The bigger you are, the more of you there is for gravity to pull. So as you grow, you weigh more pounds.

What happens in space?

When a rocket lifts a spaceship off the earth and sends it into space, gravity pulls back at the ship, balancing the pull of the ship and the astronaut trying to fly away. The balanced pulls make the ship and the astronaut inside the ship *weightless*.

The same thing happens to everything launched with a spaceship. Instruments, astronauts, food, equipment—all are affected by the balanced pulls at the same time. If not firmly fastened, they would

Pictures taken inside a special training plane. (See diagram on next page.) Astronauts (in blue) find out how it feels to be weightless.

float around. And if an astronaut stood on a scale in the spaceship, the scale would not show any weight.

Doctors are trying to discover how long a man can endure weightlessness and survive without harm.

WHY DOES AN ASTRONAUT ON HIS WAY TO SPACE FEEL HEAVY?

Can you imagine yourself sitting in a car that starts up suddenly—very, very fast? As the car pulled you forward you would feel much heavier than usual.

Sudden start

When you are traveling in a car at a steady speed, you don't feel heavier. You only feel heavy when there is a sudden spurt of speed.

The astronaut feels heavy when the rocket lifts the spaceship off the earth. He experiences such a powerful force that he can hardly turn his hands. But as soon as the rocket burns out, and is no longer accelerating him, he no longer feels heavy.

Steady speed

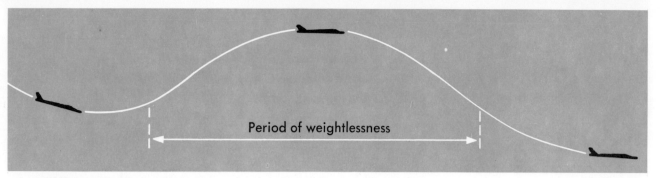

The path of a plane used to simulate weightlessness

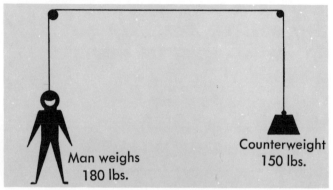

Man weighs 180 lbs.

Counterweight 150 lbs.

Man's moon weight will be one-sixth of his weight on earth. In this simulator a man who weighs 180 pounds will weigh only 30 pounds. This device, called a Peter Pan rig, makes a man feel as light as he would on the moon.

WHAT MACHINES PREPARE AN ASTRONAUT FOR FLIGHT?

Simulators are machines especially designed to give an astronaut a preview of his experiences in space.

In one simulator, a centrifuge, he is strapped to a couch and whirled. He is forced against the walls of the machine. This makes his body feel very heavy—the way he will feel during lift-off.

A trip in a powerful plane gives him a brief moment of feeling weightless. The

An astronaut in training in a centrifuge

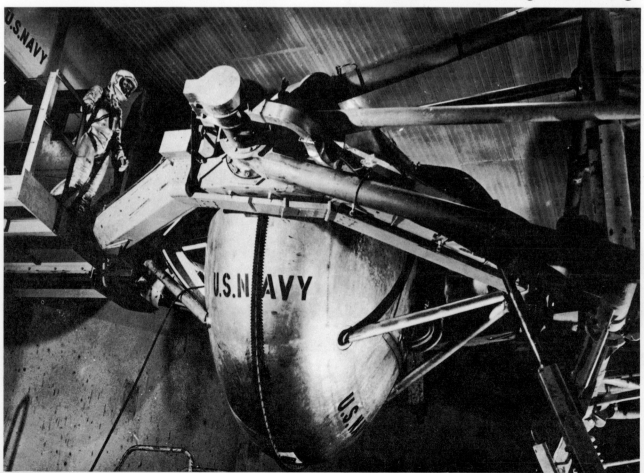

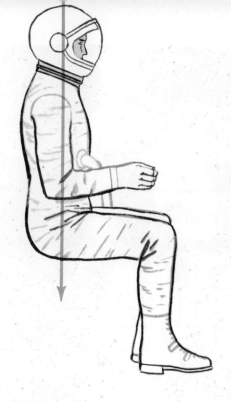

**Pressure of air is more evenly distrib-
uted over an astronaut's body when he
is lying down.**

plane makes a swift nose dive, zooms
up and flies in a long sloping path like an
orbit.

In another simulator the astronaut prac-
tices handling spaceship controls. Here,
he is strapped to a hanging couch before
a circular motion picture screen. He
watches the picture through a periscope
and works the controls.

And the astronaut also discovers what
it will be like to eat a meal in space. He
is tumbled in a fast whirling machine
while he drinks from a squeeze bottle
and eats bite-sized bits of food.

WHY DOES AN ASTRONAUT LIE DOWN DURING LIFT-OFF?

The spaceship is thrust off the earth with
tremendous force. The astronaut feels
this force. He feels a crushing weight
on his chest. He is pressed deep down
into his space couch. This experience
is a shock to a human body.

The strain and shock would be greater
for the astronaut if he stood up or sat
up. When he is lying down, the force
spreads out along the length of his body
and presses on all parts of it evenly. And
when he lies down his heart does not
have to work as hard.

An astronaut is never comfortable during the first few minutes of his flight,
but strapped down on his couch he is
better able to withstand the strain, shock
and discomfort that his body is experi-
encing.

HOW DO DOCTORS CHECK AN ASTRONAUT IN SPACE?

Small devices called sensors are fastened
to different parts of an astronaut's body.
These sensors are like the instruments
used by doctors on earth to check heart-
beats, breathing, brain waves. Reports
from these sensors are constantly being
transmitted through radio back to earth.
From these reports, doctors here on
earth learn how the body of their faraway patient is reacting in space.

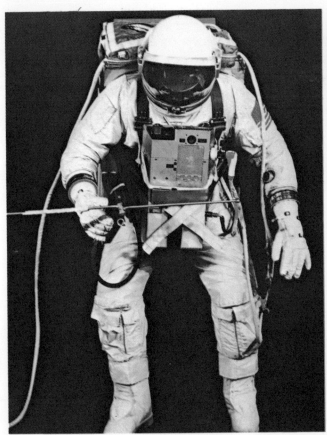

HOW DOES A SPACESUIT PROTECT AN ASTRONAUT?

An astronaut travels out to space, where there is no air. At times he travels through intense heat and cold. His spacesuit is designed to protect him and surround him with a safe atmosphere.

Every astronaut has a suit made to order for him. It may be made of nylon with a silvery coating on the outside. The coating helps to shut out the heat. The materials are airtight. They keep the air, the temperature and the pressure inside the suit as earthlike as possible.

On his back the astronaut carries a pack that serves as a combination oxygen supply, communications system and cooling unit. If he is going outside the cap-

sule, he may wear a chest pack with an emergency oxygen supply. A gold-plated visor protects the astronaut from the sun's rays.

The first spacesuits were heavy and very bulky. The astronauts could not get into them without help. A dresser was assigned to help each man dress for flight. For the Gemini 7 flight, however, astronauts Frank Borman and James A. Lovell, Jr., wore new, lightweight spacesuits. These suits were designed for comfort. They could be pressurized, but neither Borman's nor Lovell's was. (Of course the spacecraft's cabin was pressurized.) The hood on the new suit was much larger than the old helmet. But it could be unzipped and folded back during an ordinary space flight.

44

DOES AN ASTRONAUT EVER REMOVE HIS SPACESUIT DURING FLIGHT?

Unlike earlier spacesuits, the new suits designed for Gemini 7 could be taken off and stored during flight.

The crew for Apollo 7 (the first manned flight powered by a Saturn rocket) also took off their pressure suits after the first few hours of the flight. Walter Schirra and Don Eisele replaced their suits with the Apollo in-flight coveralls. These contained several pockets in which the astronauts could store small articles. Astronaut Cunningham felt more comfortable in the porous-knit cotton suit that looked like long underwear and was worn under both the pressure suit and the in-flight coveralls. All three men were wearing their pressure suits again when their spacecraft reentered the earth's atmosphere, but they came down without their helmets.

WHAT DOES AN ASTRONAUT EAT IN SPACE?

He cannot use a knife and fork the way you do. Without the force of gravity in the ship to give him weight and to give his knife weight, he would find it hard to cut meat. Moreover, the meat might float right up off the plate.

Freeze-dried foods are used in order to save space and weight. Also, they do not spoil. Because of weightlessness in space, a liquid in an open cup would form a blob that would drift around and wet anything it hit. Drinks have to be kept in plastic bags and squeezed directly into the mouth. Most other foods can be eaten with a spoon. Some of the food may be in the form of bite-sized pieces wrapped in plastic bags, but crumbly foods are a possible source of danger. Crumbs floating around the spacecraft can get into delicate instruments.

Shrimp

Beef and gravy   Peas and carrots

Chocolate pudding

With a specially designed "pistol" astronauts add water to dried foods.

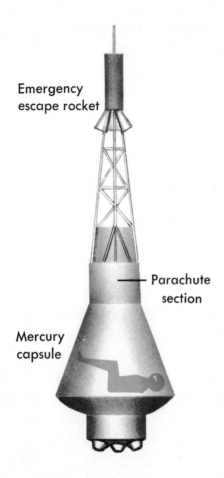

Emergency
escape rocket

Parachute
section

Mercury
capsule

ARE THERE LIFE-SAVING DEVICES IN A SPACESHIP?

There is always a chance during lift-off that a rocket will misfire. The spaceship still traveling in the earth's atmosphere would be pulled swiftly back to earth and shattered. Engineers have designed devices to rescue an astronaut if this should happen.

The escape tower is one such device. This tower is set on top of the capsule. In time of trouble, a special rocket is set off automatically or by the astronaut. It separates the capsule from the big rockets thrusting the ship out into space. The tower carries the capsule off to one side out of the path of danger.

A parachute then opens up and the capsule with the astronaut inside floats safely back to earth. If the tower is not used en route to space, it falls away from the ship when the ship reaches space.

Another safety device is the ejection seat. The astronaut is seated on it during his flight. A lever controls a hatch over the astronaut's head. The minute the lever is moved the hatch flies open. The seat with the astronaut strapped to it is shot out through the hatch into the open. Like the escape tower, the ejection seat works automatically or by hand. A device frees the astronaut from the seat, and a parachute brings him back to earth.

Once outside the capsule, the ejection seat falls away and the parachute opens, carrying the astronaut back to earth.

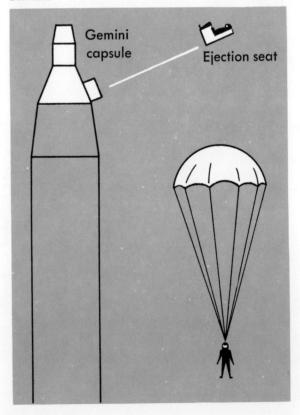

Gemini
capsule

Ejection seat

The earth turns and you turn with it. It makes one complete turn every 24 hours. Pretend that the black dot is where you live on earth.

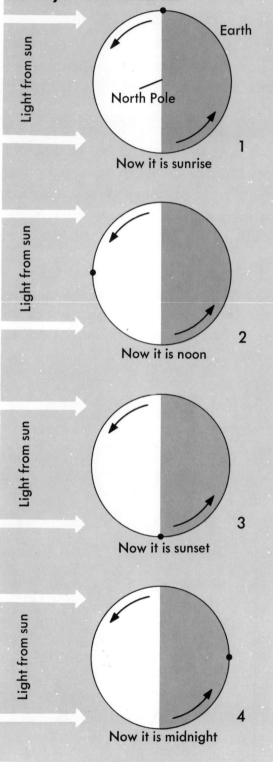

Light from sun

Earth

North Pole

1

Now it is sunrise

Light from sun

2

Now it is noon

Light from sun

3

Now it is sunset

Light from sun

4

Now it is midnight

WHY DOES AN ASTRONAUT SEE MORE THAN ONE SUNSET AND SUNRISE IN ONE DAY?

Here on earth we see just one sunrise and one sunset every twenty-four hours. We see the sunrise when the earth turns toward the sun just before our side of the earth grows bright. And we see the sunset when the earth turns away from the sun just before our side of the earth grows dark.

But the astronaut in his spaceship circles the earth many times in twenty-four hours. It may take him only an hour and a half to go all around the earth. And each time he circles the earth, he goes from the sunny side to the dark side and he sees the sun "rise" and "set."

The space between the two black dots shows how far your spot on earth moves in the last hour and a half of your 24-hour trip.

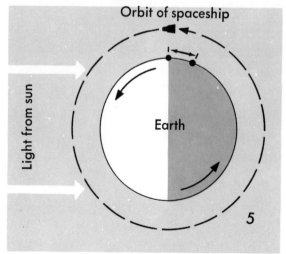

Orbit of spaceship

Light from sun

Earth

5

In the same length of time the astronaut makes one complete orbit. In 24 hours he completes 16 orbits and therefore sees 16 sunrises and 16 sunsets.

47

These two photographs, taken through a big telescope, show the side of the moon we can see.

About the Exploration of the Moon

WHY WAS THE MOON OUR FIRST GOAL IN SPACE?

The moon is nearer to the earth than any other heavenly body. (The distance varies from 221,463 miles to 252,710 miles.) The planets are much farther—many millions of miles away. If it were possible for you to travel to the moon by car at about the same speed that a car travels on a highway, it would take you approximately five months to reach the moon. But the first manned space capsule to orbit the moon reached its destination in three days. It was called Apollo 8.

Sometime in the 1980s, or later, the United States hopes to land astronauts on Mars. They will have to travel 60 million miles, and the trip could take 270 or more days.

HOW DOES THE MOON LOOK FROM EARTH?

We know the moon is very beautiful, shining above us in the dark sky. During the time of the "new moon," it looks like a slim crescent. Then gradually it becomes fat and round. As we watch it, night by night, the moon loses its roundness, becomes a crescent again and disappears. But what is the moon like from close up?

For years astronomers have studied the moon from far away through telescopes. An Italian astronomer named Galileo Galilei, in 1609, was the first man to look at the moon through a telescope. Although the telescope was not very powerful, he could see that the surface of the moon was not smooth. Instead, it was pitted with craters and dotted with highlands and mountains.

In the years since Galileo first looked at the moon through his telescope, astronomers have learned that the moon's diameter is 2,160 miles. Its gravity is only 1/6 of the earth's—not enough to retain an atmosphere. The moon has no air, no clouds and no moisture.

The moon takes 27 days, 7 hours and 43 minutes to go around the earth one time. A moon-day equals about two weeks on earth and is fiercely hot. The moon-night also lasts about two weeks and is icy cold.

49

WHAT DID UNMANNED SPACECRAFT DISCOVER ABOUT THE MOON?

Space vehicles loaded with cameras and measuring instruments brought us our first new and valuable information about the moon. They were called lunar probes. These probes took close-up pictures of the moon. In addition, they tested its surface.

Lunik II, sent out by the Russians in 1959, was the first spacecraft to crash on the moon. In July, 1964, the American space prober Ranger 7 sent back more than 4,000 pictures of the moon's surface before making a crash landing. Later Rangers sent back thousands more. Five Lunar Orbiters were launched be-tween August 10, 1966, and August 1, 1967. While orbiting the moon, they sent back nearly 2,000 photographs of its surface.

Another important American lunar probe program was the Surveyor series. These probes made soft landings on the moon instead of crashing. They tested the strength of the moon's surface and took thousands of pictures. Surveyor 7, the last of the series, carried an instrument for examining the moon's soil. Its measurements showed that the soil near the surface was apparently a fairly firm, dark material like wet sand. In places there seemed to be a thin layer of dust.

These space probes gave us much information about safe landing places for manned moon expeditions.

The Ranger and Surveyor were designed to land on the moon. (See p. 55)

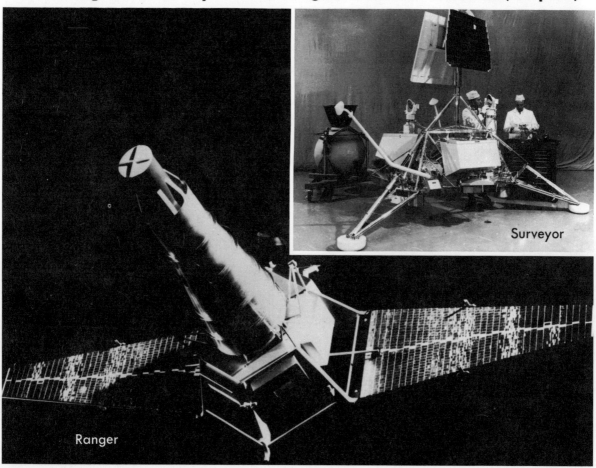

Surveyor

Ranger

Compare this picture of the moon crater, Guericke, taken from the earth (240,000 miles away) through a 100-inch telescope, with the picture below.

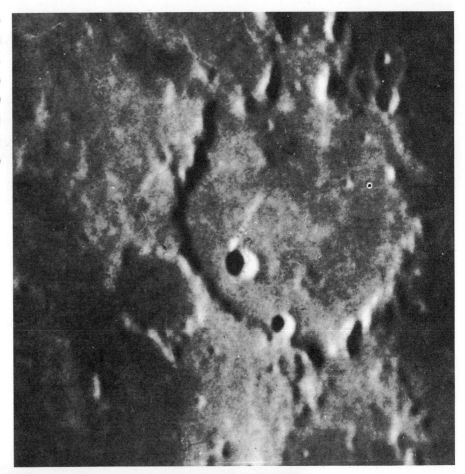

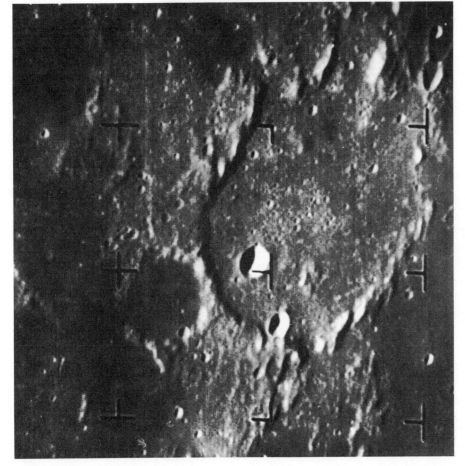

Here is the same crater photographed by Ranger 7 at a distance of 470 miles from the moon. Notice how much sharper this close-up photograph is.

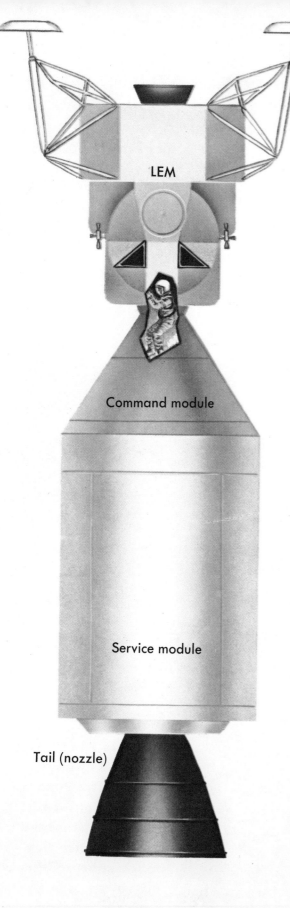

LEM

Command module

Service module

Tail (nozzle)

Astronauts crawl into LEM for moon landing. (See step 4 on opposite page.)

HOW COULD WE GET A SPACECRAFT TO THE MOON?

The first United States manned space program was Project Mercury. Its goal was to send an astronaut into orbit around the earth and find out if he could function in space. Then the astronaut and his spacecraft would be brought back to earth.

Next came Project Gemini. There were

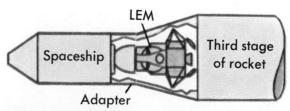

Spaceship   LEM   Third stage of rocket

Adapter

LEM rides toward moon with legs folded.

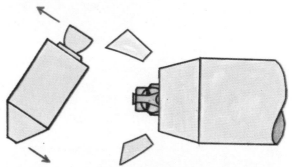

Capsule separates from spaceship and turns around.

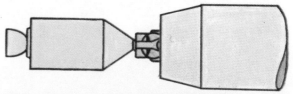

Nose-to-nose docking with LEM.

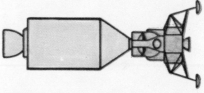

Third-stage rocket has been released. LEM's legs unfold.

two astronauts on each Gemini mission. They carried out such difficult feats as docking, or linking, their spacecraft with other orbiting spacecraft.

The final step was Project Apollo. Its goal: to land men on the moon and bring them safely back to earth.

After much discussion our scientists decided to use a powerful rocket (Saturn) to send a spaceship carrying a landing craft into orbit around the moon. An adaptor between the space capsule and the third stage of the Saturn rocket contained a moon-landing craft called LEM for Lunar Excursion Module. After the spacecraft left its earth orbit the capsule would be separated from the adaptor. The astronauts would turn the capsule around and dock with the LEM. After separating, in turn, from the adaptor, they would continue their journey until they were in moon orbit. Then two astronauts would crawl into the LEM, separate it from the mother spaceship and guide the small landing craft to a moon landing. Meanwhile the mother spaceship, manned by a third astronaut, would stay in orbit around the moon.

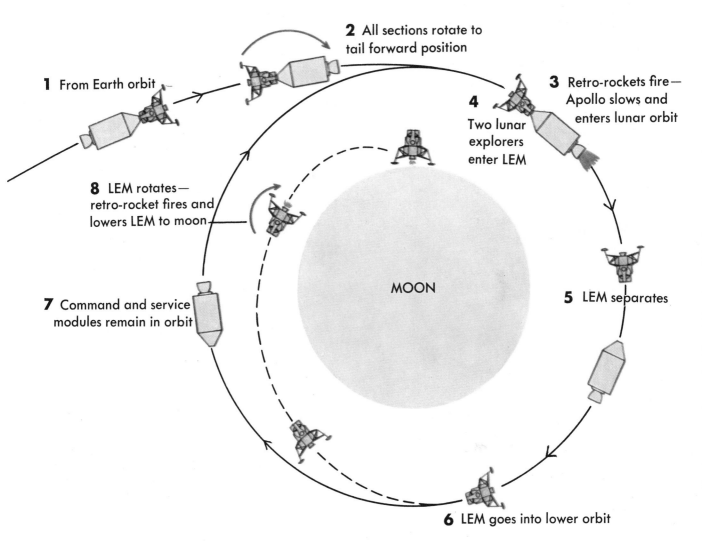

1 From Earth orbit

2 All sections rotate to tail forward position

3 Retro-rockets fire— Apollo slows and enters lunar orbit

4 Two lunar explorers enter LEM

5 LEM separates

6 LEM goes into lower orbit

7 Command and service modules remain in orbit

8 LEM rotates— retro-rocket fires and lowers LEM to moon

MOON

Apollo three-man spacecraft

WHAT IS THE APOLLO CAPSULE LIKE INSIDE?

The Apollo command module is only 12 feet, 10 inches in diameter and 10 feet, 7 inches tall. Although small, it serves as both living and working quarters for a three-man Apollo crew. During a moon mission they use it for their bedroom, kitchen, dining room, cockpit, office, laboratory and radio station. Most of the area is taken up by three reclining couches where the astronauts spend a good deal of time, but there is also room for them to stand and move around. When they are not strapped to the couches, they have to wear soft boots with soles of Velcro if they don't want to float around in the gravity-free spacecraft. The Velcro on their soles sticks to strips of the same material on the cabin floor.

The walls of the module are lined by instrument panels and consoles. Additional equipment can be stored in bays, or cupboards. There are two side windows, a hatch window and two rendezvous windows that face the module's nose. Double walls protect the astronauts from the hostile environment of space.

Apollo 9 astronauts undergo practice for takeoff in spacecraft simulator.

A Ranger spacecraft makes a planned crash landing on the moon.

The Surveyor is designed to make a soft landing on the moon.

DO ASTRONAUTS EXERCISE WHILE ON A MISSION?

Yes, it is important that they have a chance to exercise during a long flight. On the Apollo 7 mission, Astronaut Walter Cunningham reported by radio: "You start noticing that your lower abdominal muscles seem a little sore. You float around in a seated position and they kind of bunch up. After the exerciser you feel much better." He was referring to two stretchable cords attached to the wall near his feet. Lying on his back, he could do special exercises with these cords to keep his muscles in shape.

WHAT ARE CRASH LANDINGS AND SOFT LANDINGS?

Some satellites complete their job before they land. They travel with high speed and hit with great force. They are destroyed as they land. But their work has been done. Other satellites must carry out their assignments after landing. Retro-rockets slow them down so that they can make soft landings. Surveyors were designed to make soft landings on the moon.

Naturally all manned spaceships must be designed for soft landings if their passengers are to return safely to earth.

WHO WAS THE FIRST MAN TO WALK ON THE MOON?

Mission Commander Neil Armstrong of Apollo 11 was the first astronaut to set foot on the moon. Slowly and carefully he crawled backward through the hatch of the moon-landing ship, called the Eagle, and descended a ladder attached to one of the legs of the craft. As he climbed down, he exposed a camera so that the rest of his descent could be televised.

It is possible that almost a billion people throughout the world watched Armstrong take his historic first step on the moon. For the very first time a man was standing on the surface of another celestial body. It was an awe-inspiring, never-to-be-forgotten moment.

Almost at once Armstrong began to report his observations to Mission Control in Texas. "The surface is fine and powdery," he radioed. "I can pick it up loosely with my toe....I only go in a small fraction of an inch....But I can see the footprints of my boots and the treads in the fine, sandy particles."

Meanwhile, Air Force Colonel Edwin A. Aldrin, Jr., was standing by in the Eagle in case of emergency. After about 20 minutes he radioed impatiently: "Are you ready for me to come out?" Taking care not to tear his pressure suit or backpack, Aldrin descended the Eagle's ladder. He was the second man to stand on the moon's surface. "Beautiful! Beautiful!" he exclaimed as he surveyed the "moonscape."

Armstrong next mounted a 7¼-pound TV camera about 40 feet from the Eagle. Then, in full view of television spectators on earth, he unveiled a plaque which read—"Here men from the planet earth first set foot upon the moon, July 1969 A.D." (The landing took place on July 20.)

Both astronauts quickly adjusted to the weak lunar gravity. Aldrin later said: "I found that a standard loping technique of one foot in front of the other worked out quite well...One could also jump in more of a kangaroo fashion, two feet at a time."

One of Armstrong's next jobs was to plant a 3-by-5-foot American flag not far from the Eagle. Then he talked by radio to the President of the United States.

The busy astronauts had many tasks to perform on the moon. Aldrin took pictures and examined Eagle. Armstrong gathered rock samples and soil to take back to earth. He used a long-handled scoop to gather them because his pressure suit made it impossible to bend down far enough. The two men also placed scientific instruments on the moon. These would send various kinds of information to scientists on earth.

After Armstrong had been on the moon almost an hour, Mission Control radioed that it was time to return to the Eagle. The two men loaded themselves and their rock samples back on the craft. Then, after several hours of rest and preparation, they took off for their mother ship, the Columbia, manned by Air Force Lieutenant Colonel Michael Collins.

Astronaut Aldrin descends the Eagle's ladder, becoming the second man to set foot upon the moon's surface.

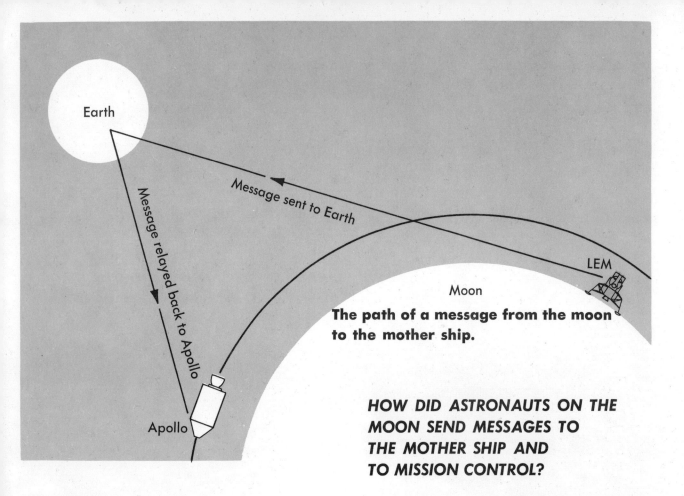

Earth

Message sent to Earth

Message relayed back to Apollo

LEM

Moon

The path of a message from the moon to the mother ship.

Apollo

WHY DID ASTRONAUTS ON THE MOON TALK TO EACH OTHER BY RADIO?

Here on earth sounds create waves in the air. When these waves reach our ears we hear the sounds. But on the moon there is no air. There can be no air waves to carry sound.

Radio waves need no air to travel. So both Neil Armstrong and Edwin Aldrin, as well as the astronauts who made the next trip to the moon in Apollo 12, talked with one another by radio. Even if they were standing right next to each other, they had to carry on their conversations by radio. They did this by using the receivers and transmitters in their backpacks.

HOW DID ASTRONAUTS ON THE MOON SEND MESSAGES TO THE MOTHER SHIP AND TO MISSION CONTROL?

When Armstrong and Aldrin spoke, tiny microphones inside their helmets transmitted their words to the communications units in their backpacks. These, in turn, sent them to a signal processor in Eagle (the LEM). By means of its own small antenna Eagle relayed a voice signal to the huge dish-shaped antenna at Goldstone, California, a quarter of a million miles away. From there it went to NASA's Goddard Space Flight Center near Washington, D.C., and then to Mission Control in Houston for rebroadcast throughout the world. It also went to Astronaut Mike Collins orbiting 69 miles above the moon in Columbia, the mother ship. Because of his position in relation to Eagle, Collins was in direct contact with the moon explorers for only a few minutes during each orbit.

HOW DID THE ASTRONAUTS GET OFF THE MOON?

The LEM (Eagle) that brought them to the moon carried them back to the mother ship. About 21 hours after landing on the moon, Neil Armstrong started up Eagle's ascent engine. "Forward 8, 7, 6, 5, abort stage, engine arm ascent, proceed. That was beautiful!" called Armstrong as Eagle's ascent stage rose from the lunar surface. Gradually Eagle maneuvered back to Columbia. When the two spacecraft swung around to the earth side of the moon on Columbia's twenty-seventh revolution, they were separated by only a few feet. Shortly after they were docked. Armstrong and Aldrin crawled through the tunnel into Columbia and Eagle was sent off into lunar orbit. On its thirty-first revolution around the moon, Columbia started up its powerful SPS engine and headed back to earth.

This is the way lunar explorers left the moon and traveled back to earth.

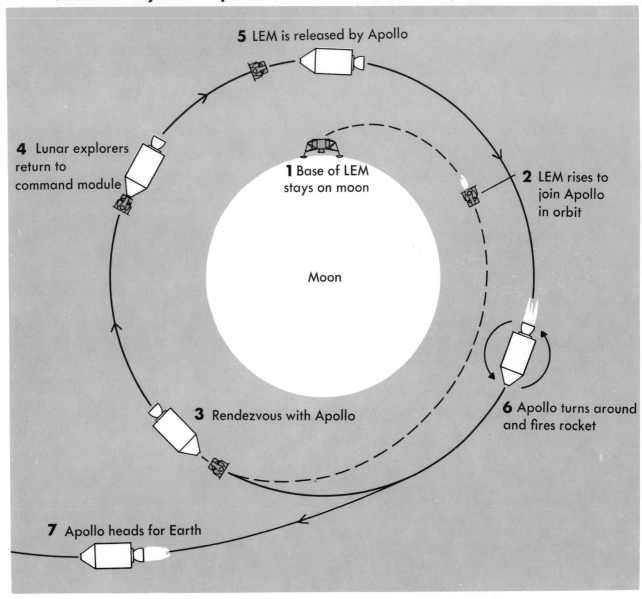

5 LEM is released by Apollo

4 Lunar explorers return to command module

1 Base of LEM stays on moon

2 LEM rises to join Apollo in orbit

Moon

3 Rendezvous with Apollo

6 Apollo turns around and fires rocket

7 Apollo heads for Earth

About Space Stations

WHAT IS A SPACE STATION?

A space station is a satellite. Orbiting in space, it will become a stopping-off place for space travelers and a home for space workers. It will have many important and different uses.

First it will be a research laboratory. Scientists will be able to do on-the-spot research with special equipment.

It will be an observatory. Space data will be collected, and photographs will be made for long-term studies.

Eventually, it will be a service station. Spare parts and fuel for spaceships will be stored there. Astronaut mechanics will be on hand to repair and refuel ships.

It will be a launching pad hundreds of miles out from earth. Satellites aimed at faraway planets will be able to start their journey beyond the atmosphere. It may also become a spaceship building yard, where prefabricated sections of satellites sent up from earth will be put together.

The space station will be a hotel, too. Astronauts will live there for a month or two at a time. They will be shuttled back and forth from earth for special jobs. And other space travelers will stop off for food, rest, recreation and help as they explore the universe.

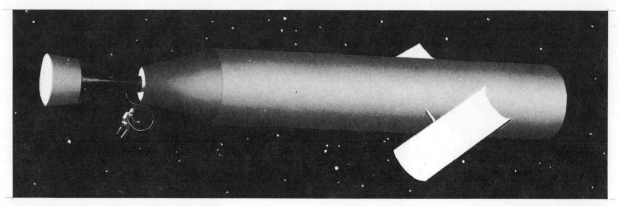

A spacecraft is docked with a space station. The astronaut is outside the ship.

WHAT WILL SPACE STATIONS LOOK LIKE?

There are a number of interesting plans for space stations. One station design looks like a gigantic wheel. The living and working quarters for men on this wheel station will be set out at the rim. The wheel will revolve to create "artificial gravity." That is, the men in the rim will be pressed toward the outer walls. They will actually be walking against the walls. But they will feel as if they are walking on a floor as they do on earth. It will be important to create "artificial gravity" in the station. Without it men might not be able to work successfully for long periods.

The stationary hub of the space station will make a good docking area. Here visiting satellites will rendezvous. And in the hub there will also be an entrance and exit for astronauts arriving and leaving the station.

HOW WILL A SPACE STATION GET OUT TO SPACE?

The first space station will probably be small. It will be sent out into an orbit in space in the same way that other satellites are sent out. A later space station will be a big one. It will be what we call a prefab building. This means that it will be built on earth and then taken apart. Its frames and chambers will be bundled, and each piece will be marked so that workers will know how to put them together. Then this huge jigsaw puzzle

The paddle-wheel space station is another design under study.

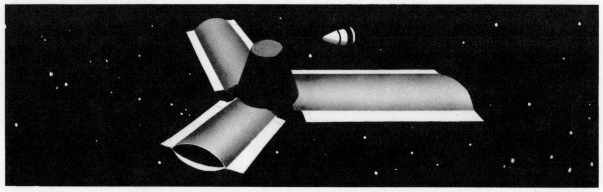

will be placed in a cargo ship and started on its journey to space.

When the cargo ship is in the proper orbit, the bundle of parts will be dumped out, into orbit and will await astronaut builders to transform it into a working space station.

HOW WILL A PREFAB SPACE STATION BE BUILT IN SPACE?

It is difficult to imagine a crew of astronauts-building a space station out in space. But a specially trained crew will study how to do the job.

The crew will be carried out in a spaceship. When the ship is in orbit near the bundle of parts for the prefab station, the men will leave the ship. They may enter smaller craft to carry them toward the bundle. But probably they will just step out into space. Because they are weightless in space they will float. They will be fastened to the ship by long cables to keep them from floating too far away.

They will steer toward the bundle with the help of spurts of gas from tiny rockets. They will wear magnetized shoes and magnetized hand grippers. They will use magnetized tools. These will be specially designed space tools. They will use a *spammer*—a space hammer. They will use a *plench*—a combined pliers and wrench, a *nab*, short for nut and bolt, and a zert, short for zero reaction tool. And so these astronaut-builders will be able to put together the pieces of the prefab space station.

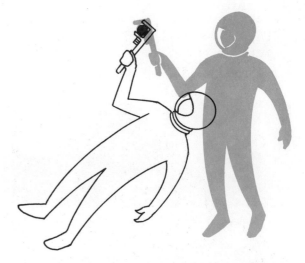

If an astronaut turned an ordinary wrench in space, his body would be turned with the same amount of force as he exerted on the wrench.

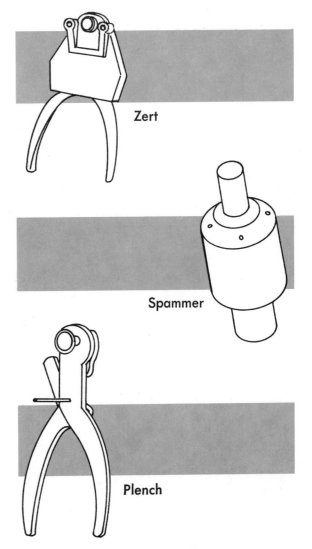

Zert

Spammer

Plench

A spaceship docks with a space station. The astronaut passes through air locks to enter the station. The spaceship then swings out of the way on a hinge, to make room for another spacecraft that is ready to dock.

WILL ASTRONAUT-BUILDERS NEED A DERRICK?

On earth the girders of a building are very heavy. But when they reach space they become weightless. This means that astronauts need not be especially strong men and that they never need a derrick to lift anything when they put together the parts of a building in space.

But astronauts have another kind of problem. They are weightless, too. Without weight they cannot push or pull anything. The girders of a space station have to be moved and fitted together. Astronaut-builders will use small rockets and spurts of gas to propel themselves. They will hold on to the girders with magnetized hand grippers. And as they move they will carry the girders along with them. They will carry the girders into position and fit them together.

HOW WILL AN ASTRONAUT ENTER A SPACE STATION?

Entering a space station will not be as easy as walking into a building on earth. In fact, the astronaut will not walk in. He will float in. He will float in because in space he is weightless.

The astronaut will enter through a trap door in the stationary hub of the station. One might call this the front door. He will float along a passageway through a series of chambers each one sealed off with air locks. These locks are there to keep the precious air inside the station if one section should leak. The astronaut will open and close the air locks carefully as he moves along. Finally when he reaches the outer rim of the station where the living and working quarters are, he will feel at home in air-conditioned rooms that have "artificial gravity."

DO YOU KNOW...

Who Was the First Space Traveler?

1957 *November 3*—The Russians sent a dog, named Laika, out to space in Sputnik II. Sputnik means companion, fellow-traveler, satellite. Laika orbited the earth 6 times and returned to earth alive. She gave proof that a living creature could survive in space.

Who Were the First Space Travelers from the United States?

1959 *December 4*—First Sam and then Miss Sam, two monkeys, were sent out on non-
1960 *January 21*—orbiting or, in space terms, suborbital flights. These flights were dress rehearsals to prepare for man's safe trip to and from space. Their chief purpose was medical. Doctors carefully checked the space travelers during their 16 minutes in flight and after their return to earth. Both Sam and Miss Sam stood the trip well.

1961 *January 31*—Ham, a chimpanzee was the next adventurer into space. He had been trained to manage levers. He managed them well during his suborbital flight of 16 minutes and proved to space officials that brain and muscle can work while weightless.

Who Was the First Human Being to Travel in Space?

1961 *April 12*—Major Yuri Gagarin, a Russian cosmonaut, astounded the world when he became the first man in space. His craft, Vostok I, a name which means East, made one complete orbit of the earth during a trip that lasted 1 hour and 48 minutes.

Who Were the First American Astronauts to Reach Space?

1961 *May 5*—Commander Alan B. Shepard was rocketed out to space in the Freedom 7. According to plan the ship did not go into orbit, and the trip lasted just 15 minutes. His flight was a test of space machinery as well as a test of human reactions to space.

1961 *July 21*—Captain Virgil I. Grissom followed Shepard in a longer trip in space of not quite 2 hours. His ship, Liberty 7, also made a planned suborbital flight. This expedition was a rechecking and further testing of man and machine in space.

Who Were the First American Astronauts to Orbit in Space?

1962 *February 20*—Colonel John Glenn in his ship, the Friendship 7, and Scott Car-
1962   *May 24*—penter, three months later in Aurora 7, made similar space flights. They both orbited the earth 3 times in not quite 5 hours. They kept in touch with tracking stations around the world and reported what they saw, how they felt and how their ships were functioning.

Who Made the First "Twin" Spaceship Flights?

1962 *August 11*—Major Adrian G. Nikolayev who was followed the next day by
1962 *August 12*—Colonel Pavel R. Popovich. In Vostok III and Vostok IV these two Russian cosmonauts traveled within 3 miles of each other. Nikolayev's ship orbited 64 times in 2 hours less than 4 days, while Popovich remained in space for not quite 3 days and his ship orbited 48 times. The successful orbiting of these ships so close to each other was a step on the way to the maneuver of rendezvousing.

Who Was the First American to Assume Complete Control of His Spaceship?

1962   *October 3*—Ten and a half minutes after launch, Commander Walter M. Schirra flipped a switch that turned off the automatic control system of his ship, the Sigma 7. This cut him off from ground control. No astronaut before him had been permitted the freedom of complete control. His ship made 6 orbits and was in flight for 9¼ hours.

Who Was the First American to Spend a Day and Night in Space?

1963   *May 15*—Major L. Gordon Cooper, Jr. remained in space in Faith 7 for 34 hours and 20 minutes. His ship orbited 22 times. Doctors were particularly interested in his ability to sleep, eat, and work during this long stretch. Cooper reported he slept comfortably for 7½ hours.

Who Was the First Woman to Travel in Space?

1963   *June 16*—A Russian, Valentina Tereshkova, made this historic flight in a "twin" spaceship trip.

1963   *June 14*—Her partner was Lt. Colonel Valery Bykovsky, who set out two days before her. Tereshkova in Vostok VI made 48 orbits during her trip of not quite 3 days. Bykovsky in Vostok V orbited 81 times in 5 days. The two ships traveled within 3 miles of each other and the two cosmonauts were in constant contact.

66

Who Made the First Three-Man Space Flight?

1964 *October 14*—A Russian crew of three cosmonauts set off in Voskhod I, a name that means sunrise in Russian. They were Colonel Vladimir M. Komarov, a qualified astronaut who piloted the ship, Konstantin P. Feoktistov, a designer-engineer-scientist, and Lt. Boris B. Yegorov, a medical doctor. These men traveled in a specially designed capsule in which they needed no spacesuits.

Who Was the First Man to Step Out of the Ship into Space?

1965 *March 18*—Colonel Aleksi A. Leonev was the daring Russian to attempt this feat. He emerged through a hatch in the Voskhod II and floated in space for 10 minutes. He was tethered to the ship by a cable. His companion Colonel Pavel I. Belayev piloted the ship. Leonev carried out this maneuver after the Voskhod II had made 13 orbits. The ship orbited 4 times more after Leonev's return. The flight lasted 26 hours.

Who Were the First Astronauts to Change the Ship's Orbit While They Were in Flight?

1965 *March 23*—Traveling in Gemini III, Commander Virgil I. Grissom and Lt. John W. Young changed both the shape and plane of orbit. This maneuver was in preparation for the rendezvous and docking operations needed for moon flights.

Who Was the First Man to Propel Himself During a "Walk" in Space?

1965 *June 2*—Major Edward A. White took a twenty-minute "walk" in space during the Gemini IV flight. While tethered to the craft he used a jet gun to propel himself.

Who Made the Longest Two-Man Space Flight?

1965 *December 4*—Astronauts Frank Borman and James A. Lovell spent 330.5 hours *to December 18*—in space in Gemini VII. Their craft landed after 206 revolutions.

Who Performed the First Docking in Space?

1966 *March 16*—Traveling in Gemini VIII, astronauts Neil A. Armstrong and David R. Scott performed the first docking in space (with Agena target vehicle).

Which Gemini Mission Produced the Record Amount of Extravehicular Activity?

1966 *November 11*—Edwin Aldrin, in Gemini XII, became the world's champion space *November 15*-walker when he took a space walk that lasted two hours and 9 minutes. Between them, he and James A. Lovell totaled a record 5 hours and 38 minutes of extravehicular activity during the flight.

Who Made the First Orbit of the Moon?

1968 *December 21*-Astronauts Frank Borman, James A. Lovell and William A. Anders in Apollo VIII made the first manned flight to vicinity of moon. They made 10 orbits of moon before returning to earth.

Which Mission Put the First LEM into Lunar Orbit?

1969 *May 18*—Apollo X put the first LEM in lunar orbit. It flew within 9.4 miles of moon's surface and inspected possible landing area.

Who Performed the Second Walk on the Moon?

1969 *November 14*-Astronauts Charles Conrad, Richard F. Gordon and Alan L. Bean flew the second lunar landing mission (Apollo XII). Conrad and Bean conducted several experiments on lunar surface.

Index

(Page numbers in bold type refer to illustrations.)

How does a satellite get out to space?

WHERE DOES SPACE BEGIN?

How does a spacesuit protect an astronaut?

Can you see a man-made satellite in space without a telescope?

HOW WILL ASTRONAUTS LEAVE THE MOON?

WHY CAN'T AN

WHAT IS A RENDEZVOUS IN SPACE?

How do communication satellites work?

Are there dangerous rays in space?

What is a satellite?

WHAT ARE CRASH LANDINGS AND SOFT LANDINGS?

WHY WILL MEN ON THE MOON TALK TO

Is there noise in space?

Why does an astronaut lie down during lift-off?

WHAT IS A PAYLOAD?

DOES AN ASTRONAUT SEE

What do we know about the moon?

What keeps a satellite from